ALTCOIN INVESTMENT STRATEGY

A Comprehensive Guide To Investing In Altcoin With Confidence

REBELLO M. POSTON

Copyright

All rights reserved. No part of this publication may be reproduced, distributed, or transmitted in any form or by any means, including photocopying, recording, or other electronic or mechanical methods, without the prior written permission of the publisher, except in the case of brief quotations embodied in critical reviews and certain other noncommercial uses permitted by copyright law.

Copyright© Rebello M. Poston, 2024.

TABLE OF CONTENTS

INTRODUCTION
- What Are Altcoins?
- The Importance of Altcoin Investment

CHAPTER 1: CRYPTOCURRENCY FUNDAMENTALS
- The Evolution of Digital Currency
- Key Differences Between Bitcoin and Altcoins
- How Blockchain Technology Works

CHAPTER 2: TYPES OF ALTCOINS
- Utility Tokens
- Security Tokens
- Stablecoins
- Governance Tokens
- Meme Coins

CHAPTER 3: STARTING YOUR ALTCOIN INVESTMENT JOURNEY
- Setting Up a Cryptocurrency Wallet
- Choosing a Reliable Exchange
- Steps to Buying Your First Altcoin

Chapter 4: INVESTMENT STRATEGIES AND TECHNIQUES
- Long-Term vs. Short-Term Investment
- Dollar-Cost Averaging
- Diversification
- Risk Management Techniques

CHAPTER 5: ANALYZING ALTCOINS
- Fundamental Analysis: Evaluating Projects and Teams
- Technical Analysis: Reading Charts and Indicators

CHAPTER 6: ADVANCED INVESTMENT METHODS
- Staking and Yield Farming
- Leveraged Trading
- Arbitrage Opportunities
- Participating in ICOs and IDOs

CHAPTER 7: MANAGING AND SECURING YOUR PORTFOLIO
- Tracking Investments and Rebalancing
- Securing Assets: Cold Storage, Two-Factor Authentication

CHAPTER 8: LEGAL, REGULATORY, AND TAX CONSIDERATIONS
- Understanding Legal Frameworks
- Tax Implications of Altcoin Investments
- Navigating Regulatory Challenges

CONCLUSION

INTRODUCTION

Altcoins, or alternative cryptocurrencies to Bitcoin, have emerged as a significant element in the evolving landscape of digital finance. These digital assets offer a myriad of opportunities for investors looking to diversify their portfolios beyond traditional investments. With thousands of altcoins available, each designed with unique features and use cases, the potential for growth and innovation in this space is immense.

Investing in altcoins can be both exhilarating and daunting. The cryptocurrency market is known for its volatility, which can lead to substantial gains but also significant losses. This book aims to demystify the world of altcoin investment, providing you with the knowledge and strategies needed to navigate this complex market confidently.

As the interest in cryptocurrencies continues to rise, understanding the nuances of altcoins becomes increasingly important. Unlike Bitcoin, which primarily serves as a store of value and a medium of exchange, altcoins can offer additional functionalities, such as smart contracts, decentralized finance (DeFi) platforms, and more. This diversification within the crypto space presents unique investment opportunities that can align with various financial goals and risk appetites.

In this book, we will explore the foundational concepts of cryptocurrencies and blockchain technology, examine the different types of altcoins, and delve into practical strategies for investing in these assets. You will learn how to conduct thorough research and analysis to identify promising altcoin projects, manage your investment portfolio effectively, and stay informed about the legal and regulatory landscape that governs this market.

Whether you are a novice investor just starting out or a seasoned trader looking to enhance your understanding, this book will serve as a comprehensive guide to altcoin investment. By the end, you will be equipped with the tools and insights needed to make informed decisions and capitalize on the opportunities that altcoins present. Let's embark on this journey into the dynamic and exciting world of altcoin investments.

WHAT ARE ALTCOINS?

Altcoins, short for "alternative coins," refer to all cryptocurrencies other than Bitcoin. Since Bitcoin's creation in 2009, it has been the dominant force in the cryptocurrency world, often referred to as digital gold. However, as the cryptocurrency market has evolved, thousands of other digital currencies have been developed, each aiming to improve upon or offer alternatives to Bitcoin's design, functionality, and application.

Altcoins vary widely in their purposes and mechanisms. Some are designed to address perceived limitations of Bitcoin, such as transaction speed, energy consumption, or scalability. Others aim to provide entirely new functionalities, such as enabling smart contracts, enhancing privacy, or facilitating decentralized finance (DeFi) applications. Ethereum, for example, is a prominent altcoin known for its smart contract capabilities, which allow developers to build decentralized applications (dApps) on its blockchain.

The altcoin market includes various categories:
1. Utility Tokens: These provide users with access to a product or service within a specific blockchain ecosystem. Ethereum's Ether (ETH) is a prime

example, as it is used to pay for transactions and computational services on the Ethereum network.

2. Security Tokens: Represent ownership in an asset, company, or other enterprise and are subject to regulatory oversight. They are often used to raise capital through Initial Coin Offerings (ICOs) or Security Token Offerings (STOs).

3. Stablecoins: Pegged to a stable asset, such as the US dollar, to minimize price volatility. Tether (USDT) and USD Coin (USDC) are popular examples.

4. Governance Tokens: Provide holders with voting rights on a project's development and operational decisions, fostering decentralized governance.

5. Meme Coins: Inspired by internet memes and often characterized by high volatility and speculative interest. Dogecoin (DOGE) is a notable example.

The vast array of altcoins offers investors numerous opportunities to explore and diversify their portfolios. Each altcoin has its unique characteristics, benefits, and risks, making it essential for investors to conduct thorough research and due diligence before investing.

THE IMPORTANCE OF ALTCOIN INVESTMENT

Investing in altcoins has become increasingly significant for several reasons, offering both diversification and growth potential within the cryptocurrency market. Here's why altcoin investment is important:

1. Diversification:
 - **Risk Management:** Diversifying into altcoins helps spread risk. While Bitcoin is often viewed as a safer, more established investment, altcoins can provide exposure to different sectors and technologies within the broader blockchain ecosystem.
   - **Reduced Dependence on Bitcoin:** The cryptocurrency market's heavy reliance on Bitcoin can lead to high volatility. By investing in altcoins, investors can mitigate risks associated with Bitcoin's price fluctuations.

2. Higher Growth Potential:
 - **Early Adoption:** Many altcoins are in the early stages of adoption and development. Investing early

in promising projects can lead to substantial returns as these projects gain traction and recognition.

   - **Innovation:** Altcoins often introduce innovative solutions to existing problems, such as faster transaction times, enhanced security features, or new financial services. Investing in these innovations can provide significant upside potential.

3. Access to Emerging Technologies:
   - **Smart Contracts and DeFi:** Altcoins like Ethereum have pioneered smart contract technology, enabling decentralized applications (dApps) and decentralized finance (DeFi) platforms. These technologies are reshaping traditional finance and creating new investment opportunities.

   - **Interoperability and Scalability:** Projects focusing on interoperability (like Polkadot) and scalability (like Solana) address some of the major limitations of earlier cryptocurrencies, paving the way for more efficient and connected blockchain ecosystems.

4. Economic and Social Impact:
   - **Financial Inclusion:** Many altcoins aim to provide financial services to underserved

populations, offering solutions like microloans, remittances, and decentralized banking. Investing in these projects can support broader social and economic development goals.

   - **Tokenization of Assets:** Altcoins facilitate the tokenization of real-world assets, from real estate to art. This can democratize access to investment opportunities and create more liquid and accessible markets.

5. Participation in Governance and Development:

   - **Decentralized Governance:** Some altcoins offer governance tokens, giving investors a voice in the project's future. This participatory approach can enhance the investor's sense of involvement and influence in the project's trajectory.

   - **Community Building:** Investing in altcoins often means joining vibrant, innovative communities that drive the projects forward. This can provide networking opportunities and deeper engagement with emerging technologies.

Altcoin investment offers a range of benefits, from diversification and growth potential to participation in cutting-edge technological developments and decentralized governance. By carefully researching and selecting altcoin projects, investors can enhance their portfolios and potentially achieve significant returns while contributing to the evolution of the digital economy.

CHAPTER 1: CRYPTOCURRENCY FUNDAMENTALS

THE EVOLUTION OF DIGITAL CURRENCY

The evolution of digital currency has been a transformative journey, reshaping the financial landscape and introducing new paradigms for value exchange. Here's an overview of this evolution:

Early Concepts and Precursors
1. Digital Cash and Cryptography (1980s-1990s):

- The concept of digital cash emerged in the 1980s, with pioneers like David Chaum, who developed DigiCash, an electronic payment system that relied on cryptographic techniques to ensure privacy.

- In the 1990s, attempts such as e-gold and Bit Gold by Nick Szabo laid the groundwork for digital currency by proposing systems that combined digital money with cryptographic security.

The Birth of Bitcoin
2. Creation of Bitcoin (2008-2009):

- The modern era of digital currency began with the publication of the Bitcoin whitepaper by the pseudonymous Satoshi Nakamoto in 2008, titled "Bitcoin: A Peer-to-Peer Electronic Cash System."

- Bitcoin's blockchain technology introduced a decentralized ledger, enabling secure and transparent transactions without the need for intermediaries. Bitcoin was launched in January 2009, marking the first successful implementation of a decentralized cryptocurrency.

Growth and Diversification
3. Emergence of Altcoins (2011-Present):

- Following Bitcoin's success, numerous alternative cryptocurrencies, or altcoins, began to emerge. Litecoin, created in 2011 by Charlie Lee, aimed to improve upon Bitcoin by offering faster transaction times and a different hashing algorithm.

- Other significant altcoins, like Ripple (XRP), introduced innovative features such as consensus algorithms for faster cross-border payments.

4. Introduction of Smart Contracts (2015):

- Ethereum, launched in 2015 by Vitalik Buterin, revolutionized the digital currency space by introducing smart contracts, self-executing contracts with the terms directly written into code. This enabled the creation of decentralized applications (dApps) and decentralized finance (DeFi) platforms.

Mainstream Adoption and Regulation

5. Increased Adoption and Institutional Interest (2017-Present):

 - The cryptocurrency market experienced significant growth and volatility in 2017, with Bitcoin reaching unprecedented highs and attracting widespread media attention. This period also saw the rise of Initial Coin Offerings (ICOs) as a fundraising mechanism for blockchain projects.

 - Institutional interest grew, with major financial institutions and companies exploring blockchain technology and investing in cryptocurrencies. Companies like Tesla and MicroStrategy made headlines with substantial Bitcoin purchases.

6. Regulatory Developments:

 - As cryptocurrencies gained popularity, regulatory bodies worldwide began to establish frameworks to govern their use. Regulations focused on preventing fraud, protecting investors, and addressing concerns related to money laundering and terrorism financing.

- Despite regulatory challenges, the increasing clarity and establishment of legal frameworks have contributed to a more mature and stable cryptocurrency market.

Technological Advancements and Future Prospects
7. Advancements in Blockchain Technology:
- Innovations in blockchain technology continue to drive the evolution of digital currencies. Projects like Polkadot and Cosmos focus on interoperability, enabling different blockchains to communicate and share information seamlessly.

- Scalability solutions, such as Ethereum 2.0 and Layer 2 protocols, aim to enhance transaction speeds and reduce costs, addressing some of the limitations of earlier blockchain networks.

8. The Rise of Central Bank Digital Currencies (CBDCs):
- Central banks worldwide are exploring the development of their own digital currencies, known as Central Bank Digital Currencies (CBDCs). These digital currencies aim to combine the benefits of digital transactions with the stability of traditional fiat currencies.

The evolution of digital currency represents a significant shift in how we perceive and handle money. From the pioneering days of cryptographic digital cash to the diverse and dynamic ecosystem of cryptocurrencies today, digital currencies have challenged traditional financial systems and opened up new possibilities for innovation and inclusion in the global economy.

KEY DIFFERENCES BETWEEN BITCOIN AND ALTCOINS

Bitcoin and altcoins, while both part of the broader cryptocurrency ecosystem, have several key differences that distinguish them in terms of purpose, technology, and market behavior. Here are the main differences:

1. Purpose and Use Case
- Bitcoin:
   - **Primary Purpose:** Bitcoin was created as a digital alternative to traditional currencies, primarily aimed at being a decentralized store of value and a medium of exchange. It is often referred to as "digital gold" due to its deflationary nature and limited supply of 21 million coins.
   - **Main Use Case:** Bitcoin's main use case is as a secure and decentralized method of transferring

value over the internet, without the need for intermediaries such as banks.

- **Altcoins:**
  - **Diverse Purposes:** Altcoins encompass a wide variety of cryptocurrencies, each designed for different purposes. Some aim to improve upon Bitcoin's shortcomings, while others offer entirely new functionalities, such as enabling smart contracts (Ethereum), providing privacy features (Monero), or powering decentralized finance (DeFi) applications.
  - **Varied Use Cases:** Altcoins can serve many use cases beyond value transfer, including decentralized applications (dApps), voting in decentralized governance, and facilitating cross-border payments.

2. Technology and Features
- **Bitcoin:**
  - **Consensus Mechanism:** Bitcoin uses a Proof-of-Work (PoW) consensus mechanism, where miners solve complex mathematical problems to validate transactions and secure the network.
  - **Blockchain Design:** Bitcoin's blockchain is relatively simple and focuses on security and decentralization, but it faces challenges with scalability and transaction speed.

- **Altcoins:**
  - **Varied Consensus Mechanisms:** Many altcoins use different consensus mechanisms, such as Proof-of-Stake (PoS), Delegated Proof-of-Stake (DPoS), or hybrid models. For example, Ethereum is transitioning from PoW to PoS with its Ethereum 2.0 upgrade.
  - **Innovative Features:** Altcoins often introduce new features and improvements. For instance, Ethereum's smart contracts enable programmable transactions, while privacy coins like Zcash and Monero offer enhanced anonymity.

3. Transaction Speed and Scalability
- **Bitcoin:**
  - **Transaction Speed:** Bitcoin's transaction speed is relatively slow, with an average block time of around 10 minutes.
  - **Scalability:** Bitcoin can handle approximately 7 transactions per second (TPS), which has led to scalability issues and higher transaction fees during periods of high demand.

- **Altcoins:**
  - **Faster Transactions:** Many altcoins are designed to offer faster transaction speeds and higher throughput. For example, Litecoin has an

average block time of 2.5 minutes, and Solana can handle thousands of TPS.

   - **Scalability Solutions:** Some altcoins implement scalability solutions such as sharding, Layer 2 protocols, and more efficient consensus algorithms to improve performance.

4. Market Behavior and Adoption
- **Bitcoin:**

   - **Market Dominance:** Bitcoin is the most widely recognized and adopted cryptocurrency, often serving as the entry point for new investors. It has the highest market capitalization and liquidity.

   - **Adoption:** Bitcoin is accepted by many merchants and is increasingly viewed as a legitimate investment by institutional investors.

- **Altcoins:**

   - **Market Volatility:** Altcoins generally exhibit higher volatility compared to Bitcoin, with prices more susceptible to market speculation and sentiment.

   - **Adoption and Use Cases:** While some altcoins have gained significant traction (e.g., Ethereum for dApps and DeFi), most have smaller market capitalizations and more niche use cases. Adoption varies widely among different altcoins.

5. Development and Governance
- **Bitcoin:**
  - **Development:** Bitcoin's development is guided by the Bitcoin Core team and a decentralized network of contributors. Changes to the protocol undergo rigorous scrutiny and community consensus.
  - **Governance:** Bitcoin's governance is relatively conservative, with a strong emphasis on maintaining security and decentralization over introducing new features.

- **Altcoins:**
  - **Development:** Altcoins often have more dynamic and flexible development environments. Projects like Ethereum have foundations or core teams that drive development and innovation.
  - **Governance:** Some altcoins use decentralized governance models, where token holders can vote on proposals and changes. For instance, governance tokens allow holders to participate in decision-making processes.

While Bitcoin remains the dominant and most established cryptocurrency, altcoins offer a wide array of innovations and improvements, catering to diverse needs and use cases within the digital economy. Understanding these differences is crucial for investors and users navigating the cryptocurrency landscape.

HOW BLOCKCHAIN TECHNOLOGY WORKS

Blockchain technology is the underlying framework that powers cryptocurrencies and many other applications by providing a decentralized, secure, and transparent way to record and transfer data. Here's a detailed explanation of how blockchain technology works:

1. Structure of a Blockchain

A blockchain is essentially a digital ledger composed of a series of blocks, each containing a list of transactions. These blocks are linked together in chronological order to form a chain.

  - **Blocks:** Each block contains three main components:
    - **Data:** The actual transactions or information stored within the block.
    - **Hash:** A unique identifier for the block, created using a cryptographic algorithm. It ensures the block's contents cannot be altered without changing the hash.

- **Previous Block Hash:** The hash of the previous block in the chain, which links the blocks together in a sequence.

2. Decentralization
Unlike traditional databases managed by a central authority, a blockchain operates on a decentralized network of computers, known as nodes. Each node maintains a copy of the entire blockchain, ensuring transparency and reducing the risk of a single point of failure.

3. Consensus Mechanisms
To add a new block to the blockchain, network participants must reach a consensus on the validity of the transactions. This is achieved through consensus mechanisms, the most common of which are Proof of Work (PoW) and Proof of Stake (PoS).

- **Proof of Work (PoW):**
  - Nodes, called miners, compete to solve complex mathematical problems. The first miner to solve the problem gets to add the new block to the blockchain and is rewarded with cryptocurrency.
  - Solving the problem requires significant computational power, which ensures security by making it difficult and expensive to alter the blockchain.

- Proof of Stake (PoS):

  - Validators are chosen to add new blocks based on the number of coins they hold and are willing to "stake" as collateral.

  - This mechanism is more energy-efficient than PoW and encourages long-term investment in the network.

4. Transaction Process

The process of recording and verifying transactions on a blockchain involves several steps:

1. Transaction Initiation: A user initiates a transaction, which is then broadcast to the network of nodes.

2. Validation: Nodes validate the transaction against the blockchain's rules (e.g., ensuring the sender has sufficient funds).

3. Block Creation: Valid transactions are grouped into a block. In PoW, miners compete to solve the cryptographic puzzle, while in PoS, validators are selected.

4. Consensus and Addition: Once a miner or validator successfully creates a new block, it is broadcast to the network. Other nodes verify the block and add it to their copy of the blockchain.

5. Confirmation: The transaction is considered confirmed once it is included in a block and several subsequent blocks, making it increasingly difficult to alter.

5. Security Features
Blockchain's security is based on several key features:

- **Cryptographic Hashing:** Each block's hash is unique and changes if any data in the block is altered, making tampering evident.
- **Decentralization:** With copies of the blockchain stored across numerous nodes, altering a single copy does not affect the entire network.
- **Consensus Mechanisms:** Reaching consensus on the validity of transactions ensures that only legitimate transactions are recorded.
- **Immutability:** Once a block is added to the blockchain, altering its data would require re-mining or re-validating all subsequent blocks, which is computationally impractical.

6. Smart Contracts
Some blockchains, like Ethereum, support smart contracts, which are self-executing contracts with the terms directly written into code. Smart contracts automatically enforce and execute

agreements when predefined conditions are met, enabling complex applications like decentralized finance (DeFi) and decentralized applications (dApps).

7. Use Cases Beyond Cryptocurrencies

Blockchain technology extends beyond cryptocurrencies, offering applications in various fields:

- **Supply Chain Management:** Tracking the origin and movement of goods.
- **Healthcare:** Securing patient records and ensuring data integrity.
- **Voting Systems:** Providing transparent and tamper-proof voting mechanisms.
- **Finance:** Enabling secure and efficient transactions and settlements.

Blockchain technology works by creating a decentralized, secure, and immutable ledger of transactions. Its combination of cryptographic hashing, decentralization, and consensus mechanisms ensures data integrity and security, making it a powerful tool for a wide range of applications.

CHAPTER 2: TYPES OF ALTCOINS

UTILITY TOKENS

Utility tokens are a type of cryptocurrency that serves a specific function within a blockchain ecosystem beyond simple value transfer. Unlike currencies such as Bitcoin or Litecoin, which primarily serve as mediums of exchange or stores of value, utility tokens are designed to provide access to products, services, or features within a decentralized platform or network. Here's a closer look at utility tokens and their key characteristics:

1. Purpose and Functionality
- **Access to Services:** Utility tokens grant holders access to specific products, services, or functionalities within a blockchain-based platform. These services can include anything from computational resources (like computing power or storage space) to access to decentralized applications (dApps), voting rights, or participation in governance mechanisms.

- **Usage Within Ecosystem:** Utility tokens are typically used as the native currency or means of exchange within the ecosystem of the platform that issues them. They serve as a medium of exchange for accessing and utilizing the platform's services and features.

2. Examples of Utility Tokens
- **Ethereum (ETH):** Ethereum's native token, Ether (ETH), is a prime example of a utility token. It is used to pay for transaction fees and computational services on the Ethereum network, such as executing smart contracts and interacting with decentralized applications.

- **Binance Coin (BNB):** Binance Coin, issued by the Binance cryptocurrency exchange, has various utilities within the Binance ecosystem. It can be used to pay for trading fees, transaction fees on Binance's decentralized exchange (DEX), participate in token sales on Binance Launchpad, and more.

- **Filecoin (FIL):** Filecoin's utility token, FIL, is used to access decentralized storage services on the Filecoin network. Users can use FIL to store or retrieve data from the decentralized storage network, with miners earning FIL as rewards for providing storage space.

3. Tokenomics and Distribution
- **Token Supply:** Utility tokens typically have a fixed or capped supply, with new tokens generated through mining, staking, or other mechanisms. The total supply of utility tokens may be distributed through a token sale (such as an Initial Coin Offering or ICO) or earned through participation in the network.

- **Token Economics:** The value of utility tokens is influenced by factors such as supply and demand dynamics within the platform's ecosystem, the utility and adoption of the platform's services, and broader market sentiment towards the cryptocurrency industry.

4. Legal and Regulatory Considerations
- **Regulatory Compliance:** Utility tokens may fall under securities regulations depending on their characteristics and how they are marketed and sold. Regulatory bodies worldwide have issued guidelines and regulations to ensure compliance with securities laws and protect investors' interests.

- **Token Utility vs. Investment Potential:** Utility tokens should primarily derive their value from their utility within the platform's ecosystem rather than speculative investment. However, investors often speculate on the potential growth and adoption of utility tokens, which can influence their market prices.

Utility tokens play a crucial role in facilitating access to decentralized platforms and services, offering holders various functionalities and benefits within blockchain ecosystems. Understanding the utility and value proposition of utility tokens is essential for investors and users looking to participate in decentralized platforms and networks.

SECURITY TOKENS

Security tokens are a type of cryptocurrency that represents ownership of an underlying asset, such as equity in a company, real estate, debt, or other investment contracts. Unlike utility tokens, which provide access to products or services within a blockchain ecosystem, security tokens are subject to securities regulations and offer investors certain rights and entitlements. Here's a closer look at security tokens and their key characteristics:

1. Representation of Ownership
- **Asset Backing:** Security tokens are backed by real-world assets, which may include equity shares

in a company, ownership of real estate properties, revenue-sharing agreements, debt instruments, or other investment contracts.

- Legal Protections: Security tokens typically represent legal ownership or rights to a specific asset, subject to the relevant securities laws and regulations governing the jurisdiction in which they are issued and traded.

2. Compliance with Regulations
- Regulatory Oversight: Security tokens are subject to securities regulations imposed by regulatory bodies such as the Securities and Exchange Commission (SEC) in the United States or the European Securities and Markets Authority (ESMA) in the European Union.

- Legal Compliance: Issuers of security tokens must comply with securities laws, including registration requirements, disclosure obligations, investor accreditation, and restrictions on trading and transferability.

3. Key Features
- Fractional Ownership: Security tokens enable fractional ownership of assets, allowing investors to purchase and trade smaller portions of high-value

assets that would otherwise be inaccessible or illiquid.

- **Automated Compliance:** Smart contracts embedded in security tokens can automate compliance with regulatory requirements, such as investor accreditation and eligibility criteria, reducing administrative overhead and operational costs.

4. Examples of Security Tokens
- **Equity Tokens:** Tokens representing ownership shares in a company, providing holders with rights to dividends, voting rights, and ownership stakes.

- **Real Estate Tokens:** Tokens backed by real estate properties, allowing investors to invest in properties and receive rental income or capital appreciation.

- **Debt Tokens:** Tokens representing debt instruments, such as bonds or loans, where investors receive periodic interest payments and repayment of principal.

5. Advantages and Challenges

- Advantages:

- **Increased Liquidity:** Security tokens can enhance liquidity for traditionally illiquid assets by enabling fractional ownership and secondary market trading.

- **Access to Global Investors:** Security token offerings (STOs) can attract a global investor base, expanding access to capital for issuers.

- **Automation and Efficiency:** Smart contracts can automate compliance and streamline processes for issuing, trading, and managing security tokens.

- Challenges:

- **Regulatory Complexity:** Compliance with securities regulations can be complex and costly, requiring issuers to navigate legal requirements across different jurisdictions.

- **Investor Education:** Investors may require education and awareness about security tokens, their rights, risks, and regulatory implications.

- **Market Fragmentation:** Fragmentation in regulatory frameworks and lack of standardization can hinder interoperability and liquidity across different security token platforms and exchanges.

Security tokens represent a bridge between traditional finance and blockchain technology, offering opportunities for asset tokenization, increased liquidity, and automation of compliance processes. While they present benefits for issuers and investors, regulatory compliance and market maturity remain key challenges for the widespread adoption of security tokens.

STABLECOINS

Stablecoins are a type of cryptocurrency designed to maintain a stable value by pegging their price to a stable asset or a basket of assets, such as fiat currencies (e.g., US dollar, euro), commodities (e.g., gold), or other cryptocurrencies. Unlike volatile cryptocurrencies like Bitcoin or Ethereum, stablecoins aim to minimize price fluctuations and provide stability, making them suitable for various use cases, including payments, remittances, and hedging against cryptocurrency market volatility. Here's a closer look at stablecoins and their key characteristics:

1. Stability Mechanisms
- **Fiat-Collateralized:** Fiat-collateralized stablecoins are backed by reserves of fiat currency held in bank accounts or custodian accounts. Each stablecoin in circulation is backed by an equivalent

amount of fiat currency held in reserve, ensuring a 1:1 peg to the underlying asset.

- **Crypto-Collateralized:** Crypto-collateralized stablecoins are backed by cryptocurrencies held as collateral. Smart contracts and algorithms maintain the stability of the stablecoin's value by dynamically adjusting the collateralization ratio and issuing or burning tokens based on market demand.

- **Algorithmic:** Algorithmic stablecoins use algorithmic mechanisms to regulate the stablecoin's supply and demand dynamically. These stablecoins rely on algorithmic governance and mechanisms such as seigniorage shares or rebasing to maintain price stability.

2. Use Cases
- **Payments and Remittances:** Stablecoins provide a reliable and efficient medium of exchange for payments and remittances, offering fast settlement times and low transaction fees compared to traditional banking systems.

- **Hedging Against Volatility:** Traders and investors use stablecoins as a hedge against cryptocurrency market volatility. By converting volatile cryptocurrencies into stablecoins during market downturns, investors can preserve value and mitigate losses.

- **Decentralized Finance (DeFi):** Stablecoins play a central role in decentralized finance (DeFi) applications, serving as the primary unit of account and medium of exchange within DeFi protocols for lending, borrowing, yield farming, and liquidity provision.

3. Regulatory Considerations
- **Compliance and Regulation:** Stablecoin issuers must comply with regulatory requirements, including anti-money laundering (AML) and know-your-customer (KYC) regulations, to ensure legal compliance and mitigate regulatory risks.

- **Reserve Audits:** Fiat-collateralized stablecoins often undergo regular audits by independent third-party firms to verify the reserves' existence and ensure transparency and trust among users.

4. Examples of Stablecoins
- **Tether (USDT):** Tether is one of the most widely used fiat-collateralized stablecoins, pegged to the US dollar on a 1:1 basis. It operates on various blockchain networks, including Ethereum and Tron.

- **USD Coin (USDC):** USD Coin is another popular fiat-collateralized stablecoin backed by US dollars held in reserve by regulated financial institutions. It is governed by the Centre Consortium, a collaboration between Circle and Coinbase.

- **Dai (DAI):** Dai is a decentralized stablecoin issued on the Ethereum blockchain and collateralized by cryptocurrencies locked in smart contracts within the MakerDAO protocol. It maintains its stability through algorithmic mechanisms and decentralized governance.

5. Advantages and Challenges

- **Advantages:**
   - **Stability:** Stablecoins offer price stability, making them suitable for everyday transactions and financial applications.
   - **Accessibility:** Stablecoins enable global access to digital assets, financial services, and decentralized applications, regardless of geographical location or banking infrastructure.
   - **Efficiency:** Stablecoins facilitate fast and low-cost transactions, enabling seamless value transfer across borders and reducing reliance on traditional banking systems.

- **Challenges:**
  - **Regulatory Uncertainty:** Stablecoins face regulatory scrutiny and uncertainty, particularly regarding their classification, compliance requirements, and potential systemic risks.
  - **Centralization Risks:** Fiat-collateralized stablecoins may pose centralization risks if issuers do not maintain adequate reserves or transparency, potentially leading to counterparty risks and loss of trust.
  - **Market Liquidity:** Algorithmic stablecoins may face challenges related to market liquidity and stability during periods of high volatility or market stress, raising concerns about their reliability as a store of value.

Stablecoins offer a reliable and efficient means of transacting and storing value in the digital economy, with applications spanning payments, remittances, decentralized finance, and more. While stablecoins present significant advantages, regulatory compliance, centralization risks, and market liquidity remain key considerations for their widespread adoption and long-term viability.

GOVERNANCE TOKENS

Governance tokens are a type of cryptocurrency that grants holders the right to participate in the governance and decision-making processes of a decentralized protocol, platform, or organization. Unlike traditional cryptocurrencies, which primarily serve as a medium of exchange or store of value, governance tokens enable token holders to influence the direction, development, and operation of the underlying decentralized network. Here's a closer look at governance tokens and their key characteristics:

1. Purpose and Functionality

- **Participation in Governance:** Governance tokens empower holders to propose, discuss, and vote on changes to the protocol's parameters, such as upgrades, parameter adjustments, fee changes, and policy decisions.

- **Decentralized Decision-Making:** Governance tokens facilitate decentralized governance, allowing token holders to collectively govern the protocol without relying on centralized authorities or intermediaries.

2. Governance Mechanisms

- **Proposal Submission:** Token holders can submit proposals for protocol changes or improvements, which are then open for discussion and voting by the community.

- **Voting Rights:** Holders of governance tokens have voting rights proportional to their token holdings, allowing them to vote on proposals and governance decisions.

- **Delegated Voting:** In some governance systems, token holders can delegate their voting rights to other participants or entities, known as delegates or proxies, to vote on their behalf.

3. Examples of Governance Tokens

- **Compound (COMP):** Compound is a decentralized lending protocol that issues the COMP token to stakeholders. COMP holders can propose and vote on changes to the protocol, including adding or removing supported assets, adjusting interest rates, and modifying protocol parameters.

- **Uniswap (UNI):** Uniswap is a decentralized exchange (DEX) protocol that introduced the UNI token to its community. UNI holders can participate in governance by proposing and voting on changes to the protocol, such as fee adjustments, liquidity incentives, and protocol upgrades.

- **MakerDAO (MKR):** MakerDAO is a decentralized autonomous organization (DAO) that governs the Maker Protocol and issues the MKR token. MKR holders participate in key governance decisions, including managing the stability fee, collateral types, and risk parameters of the Dai stablecoin.

4. Tokenomics and Distribution

- **Token Distribution:** Governance tokens are typically distributed through various mechanisms, including token sales, airdrops, liquidity mining, and community incentives.

- **Token Utility:** Governance tokens derive their value from their utility in governing the protocol and participating in decision-making processes. The more actively engaged the community is in governance, the more valuable the governance token may become.

5. Advantages and Challenges

- **Advantages:**

    - **Decentralized Governance:** Governance tokens enable decentralized decision-making, fostering community engagement and ownership of the protocol.

    - **Flexibility and Adaptability:** Governance tokens allow protocols to adapt and evolve over time by incorporating feedback and proposals from the community.

    - **Alignment of Incentives:** Governance token holders have a vested interest in the protocol's success and sustainability, aligning incentives between token holders and protocol developers.

- **Challenges:**

    - **Participation and Engagement:** Ensuring broad participation and engagement in governance processes can be challenging, as it requires active involvement and coordination among token holders.

    - **Governance Sybil Attacks:** Governance tokens may be susceptible to governance Sybil attacks, where a single entity accumulates a majority of tokens to control decision-making processes.

    - **Governance Efficiency and Effectiveness:** Balancing decentralization with efficiency and effectiveness in governance processes requires careful design and experimentation with governance mechanisms.

Governance tokens play a critical role in decentralized governance, enabling token holders to collectively govern and shape the direction of decentralized protocols and organizations. While governance tokens offer significant advantages in fostering community engagement and ownership, they also pose challenges related to participation, governance efficiency, and coordination among stakeholders. Continued innovation and experimentation with governance mechanisms are essential for the long-term sustainability and success of decentralized governance models.

MEME COINS

Meme coins, also known as meme cryptocurrencies or meme tokens, are a type of cryptocurrency that gain popularity primarily through social media, online communities, and internet memes. Unlike traditional cryptocurrencies, which often have underlying technology or utility, meme coins are characterized by their humorous or satirical nature and often lack fundamental value or utility beyond their entertainment value. Here's a closer look at meme coins and their key characteristics:

1. Origins and Culture
- **Internet Culture:** Meme coins originate from internet culture and communities, often drawing inspiration from internet memes, jokes, or viral trends. They are created and promoted by internet users, communities, or influencers for entertainment purposes rather than serious investment or technological innovation.

- **Community-Driven:** Meme coins thrive on community engagement and participation, with enthusiasts sharing memes, jokes, and content related to the coin on social media platforms, forums, and chat groups.

2. Characteristics

- Humorous or Satirical Themes: Meme coins often feature humorous or satirical themes in their branding, logos, and marketing materials. They may parody or reference popular memes, celebrities, or cultural phenomena.

- Lack of Utility or Fundamental Value: Unlike traditional cryptocurrencies that may have underlying technology, use cases, or utility, meme coins typically lack fundamental value or utility beyond their entertainment value. They may not serve any practical purpose other than being a vehicle for internet jokes and speculation.

3. Pump and Dump Dynamics

- Speculative Nature: Meme coins are often subject to speculative trading and volatility, driven by hype, sentiment, and social media trends. Prices can experience rapid fluctuations based on viral marketing campaigns or online discussions.

- Pump and Dump Schemes: Some meme coins may be susceptible to pump and dump schemes, where promoters artificially inflate the price of the coin through coordinated buying and hype, only to sell off their holdings at a profit, leaving unsuspecting investors with losses.

4. Examples of Meme Coins
- **Dogecoin (DOGE):** Dogecoin is one of the earliest and most well-known meme coins, featuring the Shiba Inu dog from the "Doge" internet meme. Despite its origins as a joke, Dogecoin gained a dedicated community and became widely traded and accepted as a form of payment.

- **Shiba Inu (SHIB):** Shiba Inu is another meme coin inspired by the Doge meme, featuring the same breed of dog. It gained popularity in 2021, driven by viral marketing and social media hype.

- **SafeMoon (SAFEMOON):** SafeMoon gained attention for its unique tokenomics, which include mechanisms such as static rewards, automatic liquidity pools, and manual burns. It garnered a large following on social media platforms but also faced criticism for its lack of transparency and risks associated with its tokenomics.

5. Risks and Considerations
- **Speculative Investment:** Investing in meme coins carries significant risks due to their speculative nature, lack of fundamentals, and susceptibility to market manipulation. Investors

should exercise caution and conduct thorough research before investing in meme coins.

- **Volatility and Price Fluctuations:** Meme coins are highly volatile, with prices subject to rapid fluctuations based on social media trends, news, and market sentiment. Investors should be prepared for the possibility of substantial gains or losses in a short period.

- **Community and Sentiment Risks:** Meme coins rely heavily on community engagement and sentiment. Negative news, controversies, or changes in sentiment within the community can have a significant impact on the coin's price and reputation.

Meme coins are a unique phenomenon within the cryptocurrency space, driven by internet culture, humor, and social media trends. While they offer entertainment value and speculative trading opportunities, investors should approach meme coins with caution and be aware of the associated risks, including volatility, market manipulation, and lack of fundamental value.

CHAPTER 3: STARTING YOUR ALTCOIN INVESTMENT JOURNEY

SETTING UP A CRYPTOCURRENCY WALLET

Setting up a cryptocurrency wallet is essential for securely storing, sending, and receiving cryptocurrencies. Here's a step-by-step guide to setting up a cryptocurrency wallet:

1. Choose a Wallet Type

- **Hardware Wallet:** Hardware wallets are physical devices that store your cryptocurrency keys offline, providing the highest level of security. Popular hardware wallets include Ledger Nano S, Ledger Nano X, and Trezor.

- **Software Wallet:** Software wallets are applications or programs that run on your computer, smartphone, or tablet. They are convenient for everyday use but may be less secure than hardware wallets. Examples include Exodus, Atomic Wallet, and Trust Wallet.

- **Online/Web Wallet:** Online wallets are hosted on the internet by cryptocurrency exchanges or wallet service providers. While convenient, they are more susceptible to hacking and security breaches. Examples include Coinbase, Binance, and Blockchain.com.

2. Download and Install the Wallet

- **Hardware Wallet:** If you've chosen a hardware wallet, follow the manufacturer's instructions to set it up. This typically involves connecting the device to your computer or smartphone and installing the necessary software.

- **Software Wallet:** Visit the official website or app store of the chosen software wallet and download the application compatible with your device's operating system (e.g., Windows, macOS, iOS, Android).

- **Online/Web Wallet:** Visit the website of the chosen online wallet provider and sign up for an account. Follow the registration process and set up two-factor authentication (2FA) for added security.

3. Create a New Wallet

- **Hardware Wallet:** Once the hardware wallet is set up, follow the on-screen instructions to generate a new wallet. You may be prompted to create a PIN code and write down a recovery seed phrase, which is crucial for restoring your wallet if the device is lost or damaged.

- **Software Wallet:** Open the downloaded software wallet application and follow the on-screen instructions to create a new wallet. You will typically be asked to choose a strong password and write down a recovery seed phrase.

- **Online/Web Wallet:** Log in to your newly created online wallet account and follow the on-screen instructions to set up your wallet. You may be prompted to enable additional security features, such as 2FA, and verify your identity.

4. Backup Your Wallet
- **Hardware Wallet:** Write down the recovery seed phrase provided during setup and store it in a safe and secure location. This recovery phrase is crucial for recovering access to your funds if your hardware wallet is lost, stolen, or damaged.

- **Software Wallet:** Write down the recovery seed phrase provided during setup and store it securely offline. Do not share this phrase with anyone else, as it can be used to access your funds.

- **Online/Web Wallet:** Enable two-factor authentication (2FA) for added security. This typically involves linking your wallet account to an authenticator app on your smartphone or receiving authentication codes via SMS or email.

5. Fund Your Wallet

- **Hardware Wallet:** Connect your hardware wallet to your computer or smartphone and follow the instructions to access your wallet receiving address. Transfer cryptocurrency from an exchange or another wallet to this address.

- **Software Wallet:** Open your software wallet application and navigate to the "Receive" or "Receive Funds" section. Copy your wallet's receiving address and use it to receive cryptocurrency from an exchange or another wallet.

- **Online/Web Wallet:** Log in to your online wallet account and navigate to the "Deposit" or "Receive" section. Copy your wallet receiving address and use it to receive cryptocurrency from an exchange or another wallet.

6. Secure Your Wallet

- **Hardware Wallet:** Keep your hardware wallet safe and secure, preferably in a physical safe or secure location. Avoid sharing your PIN code or recovery seed phrase with anyone else.

- **Software Wallet:** Keep your software wallet application up to date with the latest security patches and updates. Enable additional security features such as biometric authentication or PIN code protection.

- **Online/Web Wallet:** Enable two-factor authentication (2FA) for added security. Be cautious of phishing attempts and only access your online wallet through the official website or app.

By following these steps, you can set up a cryptocurrency wallet and securely store your digital assets. Remember to keep your wallet and recovery seed phrase safe and never share them with anyone else.

CHOOSING A RELIABLE EXCHANGE

Choosing a reliable cryptocurrency exchange is crucial for securely buying, selling, and trading cryptocurrencies. Here are some factors to consider when selecting a reliable exchange:

1. Security
- **Regulation and Compliance:** Look for exchanges that are regulated and compliant with relevant laws and regulations in their jurisdiction. Regulatory oversight adds an extra layer of security and protection for users' funds.

- **Security Measures:** Check what security measures the exchange has in place, such as two-factor authentication (2FA), cold storage for user funds, encryption protocols, and regular security audits.

- **Track Record:** Research the exchange's track record for security incidents, hacks, and breaches. Choose exchanges with a history of prioritizing security and implementing robust security measures.

2. Reputation
- **User Reviews and Feedback:** Read reviews and feedback from other users to gauge their

experiences with the exchange. Look for patterns of positive or negative feedback regarding security, customer support, fees, and ease of use.

- **Industry Recognition:** Consider exchanges that have received industry recognition and awards for their services and security practices. Reputable exchanges often receive positive recognition from industry experts and publications.

3. Liquidity
- **Trading Volume:** High trading volume indicates liquidity, which is essential for executing trades quickly and at favorable prices. Choose exchanges with sufficient liquidity in the cryptocurrencies you intend to trade.

- **Supported Cryptocurrencies:** Check the exchange's list of supported cryptocurrencies to ensure it offers a diverse range of assets for trading and investment.

4. Fees
- **Trading Fees:** Evaluate the exchange's fee structure for trading, deposits, withdrawals, and other services. Look for transparent fee schedules and competitive rates compared to other exchanges.

- **Fee Discounts:** Some exchanges offer fee discounts or incentives for high-volume traders, market makers, or users who hold native exchange tokens.

5. User Experience
- **Interface and Design:** Choose exchanges with user-friendly interfaces and intuitive design that make it easy to navigate and execute trades. Look for features such as advanced charting tools, order types, and customization options.

- **Customer Support:** Consider the quality and responsiveness of the exchange's customer support. Look for exchanges that offer multiple channels of support, such as live chat, email, or phone support, and have a reputation for timely resolution of customer inquiries and issues.

6. Geographic Availability
- **Supported Countries:** Ensure that the exchange operates in your country or region and supports users from your geographic location. Some exchanges have restrictions or limitations on users from certain countries due to regulatory reasons.

- **Payment Methods:** Check the supported payment methods for depositing and withdrawing funds. Choose exchanges that offer convenient and accessible payment options compatible with your banking system or preferences.

7. Additional Features
- **Mobile App:** Consider whether the exchange offers a mobile app for trading on the go. A mobile app provides flexibility and convenience for managing your cryptocurrency portfolio from your smartphone or tablet.

- **Educational Resources:** Some exchanges offer educational resources, tutorials, and tools to help users learn about cryptocurrency trading, market analysis, and investment strategies. Look for exchanges that prioritize user education and empowerment.

By considering these factors and conducting thorough research, you can choose a reliable cryptocurrency exchange that meets your needs and preferences for trading and investing in cryptocurrencies. Remember to start with small amounts when testing out a new exchange and always prioritize security and transparency when handling your funds.

STEPS TO BUYING YOUR FIRST ALTCOIN

Buying your first altcoin can be an exciting venture, but it's essential to approach it with caution and thorough research. Here are the steps to help you purchase your first altcoin:

1. Research and Choose an Altcoin
- **Market Research:** Research different altcoins to identify ones that align with your investment goals, risk tolerance, and preferences. Consider factors such as the project's technology, team, use case, market potential, and community support.

- **Due Diligence:** Conduct thorough due diligence on the altcoin you're considering investing in. Review the project's whitepaper, roadmap, development progress, social media presence, and community engagement to assess its credibility and potential for growth.

2. Select a Reliable Cryptocurrency Exchange
- **Choose an Exchange:** Select a reputable cryptocurrency exchange that supports the altcoin you want to buy. Consider factors such as security,

fees, liquidity, supported payment methods, and geographic availability.

- **Create an Account:** Sign up for an account on the chosen exchange and complete the account verification process, which may involve providing personal information and identity verification documents.

3. Deposit Funds into Your Exchange Account

- **Deposit Fiat Currency:** Deposit fiat currency (e.g., USD, EUR) into your exchange account using supported payment methods such as bank transfer, credit/debit card, or electronic payment services.

- **Deposit Cryptocurrency:** Alternatively, if you already own cryptocurrencies such as Bitcoin or Ethereum, you can deposit them into your exchange account to use for purchasing the altcoin.

4. Place an Order to Buy the Altcoin

- **Navigate to the Trading Section:** Go to the trading section or marketplace on the exchange platform and locate the trading pair for the altcoin you want to buy (e.g., ALT/BTC, ALT/ETH).

- **Choose Order Type:** Select the type of order you want to place, such as a market order (executed at the current market price) or a limit order (set at a specific price).

- **Enter Order Details:** Enter the amount of the altcoin you want to buy and review the order details, including the price and total cost. Confirm the order to execute the trade.

5. Securely Store Your Altcoin
- **Transfer to Wallet:** Once your purchase is complete, consider transferring your altcoins from the exchange to a secure cryptocurrency wallet for long-term storage. Hardware wallets offer the highest level of security, followed by software wallets and online wallets.

- **Backup Recovery Phrase:** If you're using a software or hardware wallet, ensure you back up the recovery phrase provided during wallet setup. Store this phrase securely offline, as it can be used to restore access to your wallet if needed.

6. Monitor Your Investment
- **Stay Informed:** Stay informed about market developments, news, and updates related to the altcoin you've invested in. Follow the project's

official channels, social media accounts, and community forums for updates and announcements.

- Monitor Price Movements: Keep an eye on the price movements of your altcoin investment to track its performance over time. Use cryptocurrency tracking websites or portfolio management apps to monitor your investment portfolio.

By following these steps and conducting thorough research, you can purchase your first altcoin with confidence and embark on your journey into the world of cryptocurrency investing. Remember to invest only what you can afford to lose and to practice risk management strategies to mitigate potential losses.

Chapter 4: INVESTMENT STRATEGIES AND TECHNIQUES

LONG-TERM VS. SHORT-TERM INVESTMENT

When it comes to investing in cryptocurrencies, as with any other asset class, you can choose between long-term and short-term investment strategies. Here's a breakdown of the differences between the two:

Long-Term Investment
- **Strategy:** Long-term investment involves buying and holding assets for an extended period, typically years or even decades.

- **Goal:** The primary goal of long-term investment is to capitalize on the potential growth and value appreciation of the asset over time.

- **Benefits:**
  - **Potential for Higher Returns:** Long-term investors aim to benefit from the overall growth trajectory of the cryptocurrency market, which

historically has shown significant appreciation over time.

  - **Reduced Stress:** Long-term investors are less concerned with short-term price fluctuations and market volatility, as their focus is on the asset's long-term fundamentals and potential.

  - **Tax Benefits:** In some jurisdictions, long-term capital gains are taxed at a lower rate than short-term gains, providing tax advantages for investors who hold their assets for an extended period.

- **Considerations:**

  - **Volatility Tolerance:** Long-term investors must be comfortable with the inherent volatility of the cryptocurrency market and prepared to weather periods of price volatility without panic selling.

  - **Research and Due Diligence**: Thorough research and due diligence are essential for identifying promising projects with strong fundamentals and long-term potential.

Short-Term Investment (Trading)

- **Strategy:** Short-term investment, also known as trading, involves buying and selling assets within a relatively short time frame, ranging from minutes to days or weeks.

- **Goal:** The primary goal of short-term investment is to profit from short-term price fluctuations and market trends, regardless of the asset's long-term fundamentals.

- **Benefits:**
  - **Liquidity and Flexibility:** Short-term traders can capitalize on short-term price movements and market opportunities, potentially generating quick profits.
  - **Adaptability:** Short-term traders can adjust their strategies and positions based on changing market conditions, news events, and technical indicators.
  - **Diversification:** Short-term trading allows investors to diversify their trading strategies and portfolios across multiple assets, markets, and trading pairs.

- **Considerations:**
  - **Risk Management:** Short-term trading carries higher risks due to the increased volatility and uncertainty associated with short-term price movements. Traders must implement robust risk management strategies to protect their capital.
  - **Time and Effort:** Short-term trading requires active monitoring of the market, technical analysis,

and execution of trades, which can be time-consuming and mentally demanding.

- **Emotional Discipline:** Successful short-term trading requires emotional discipline, patience, and the ability to control emotions such as greed and fear.

Choosing the Right Strategy
- **Investment Goals:** Consider your investment goals, risk tolerance, time horizon, and financial situation when choosing between long-term and short-term investment strategies.

- **Diversification:** Some investors may choose to employ a combination of long-term and short-term investment strategies to diversify their portfolios and balance risk and return.

- **Education and Experience:** Both long-term and short-term investment strategies require knowledge, education, and experience to execute successfully. Invest time in learning about the cryptocurrency market, investment principles, and trading strategies before making investment decisions.

Ultimately, whether you choose a long-term or short-term investment strategy depends on your individual preferences, goals, and risk tolerance. Both approaches have their pros and cons, and there is no one-size-fits-all solution. It's essential to conduct thorough research, develop a clear investment plan, and stay disciplined in executing your strategy to achieve your investment objectives.

DOLLAR-COST AVERAGING

Dollar-cost averaging (DCA) is an investment strategy that involves investing a fixed amount of money at regular intervals, regardless of the asset's price. Here's how dollar-cost averaging works and its benefits:

How Dollar-Cost Averaging Works:

1. Regular Investments: Under the DCA strategy, you invest a fixed amount of money (e.g., $100) at regular intervals (e.g., weekly, monthly) into a particular asset, such as a cryptocurrency.

2. Price Variability: Since you're investing at regular intervals, you'll buy more of the asset when prices are low and less when prices are high. This approach helps smooth out the impact of price volatility over time.

3. Averaging Out: Over time, the average cost of your investments tends to decrease because you're buying more units of the asset when prices are low and fewer units when prices are high.

4. Long-Term Accumulation: Dollar-cost averaging is typically used for long-term accumulation of assets, allowing investors to gradually build their investment portfolio over time.

Benefits of Dollar-Cost Averaging:
1. Reduced Market Timing Risk: DCA helps reduce the risk of mistiming the market by spreading out investments over time. Instead of trying to predict market highs and lows, you're consistently investing regardless of short-term price fluctuations.

2. Discipline and Consistency: DCA instills discipline and consistency in your investment approach, as you're investing regularly regardless of market conditions. This can help prevent emotional decision-making and impulsive reactions to market volatility.

3. Lower Average Cost: Over time, the average cost of your investments tends to be lower compared to investing a lump sum at a single point in time. This is because DCA allows you to buy more units of the asset when prices are low.

4. Reduced Psychological Stress: DCA can help reduce psychological stress and anxiety associated with investing, as you're less focused on short-term price movements and more on long-term wealth accumulation.

5. Automated Investing: Many brokerage platforms and investment accounts offer automated DCA features, allowing you to set up recurring investments at regular intervals without the need for manual intervention.

Considerations for Dollar-Cost Averaging:
1. Asset Selection: DCA can be applied to various assets, including stocks, bonds, mutual funds, and cryptocurrencies. Consider the asset's long-term growth potential, volatility, and risk factors when implementing DCA.

2. Investment Horizon: DCA is best suited for investors with a long-term investment horizon who are willing to hold their investments for an extended period. Short-term traders may prefer other strategies tailored to their investment goals and timeframes.

3. Costs and Fees: Be mindful of any transaction costs or fees associated with DCA, as these can impact your overall returns over time. Choose investment platforms with low fees to maximize the benefits of DCA.

Overall, dollar-cost averaging is a simple yet effective investment strategy for building wealth gradually over time while minimizing market timing risk and psychological stress. By staying disciplined, consistent, and focused on your long-term goals, you can harness the power of DCA to achieve financial success.

DIVERSIFICATION

Diversification is a risk management strategy that involves spreading investments across different assets, industries, sectors, or geographic regions to reduce the overall risk of a portfolio. Here's why diversification is important and how to implement it effectively:

Importance of Diversification:

1. Risk Reduction: Diversification helps mitigate the impact of individual asset or market volatility on your overall investment portfolio. By spreading investments across diverse assets, you reduce the risk of significant losses from any single investment.

2. Stable Returns: Diversification aims to create a more stable and consistent return profile for your portfolio over time. While some assets may experience fluctuations or downturns, others may perform well, balancing out the overall returns.

3. Opportunity Capture: Diversification allows you to capitalize on opportunities in different asset classes or sectors that may be performing well at different times. By diversifying, you're not overly reliant on the performance of any single asset or market.

4. Risk-Return Tradeoff: Diversification enables you to achieve a balance between risk and return that aligns with your investment goals, risk tolerance, and time horizon. By diversifying, you can potentially optimize the risk-return tradeoff for your portfolio.

Implementing Diversification:
1. Asset Allocation: Allocate your investment capital across different asset classes, such as stocks, bonds, real estate, commodities, and cryptocurrencies. Each asset class has its own risk-return characteristics, providing diversification benefits.

2. Sector and Industry Allocation: Within each asset class, diversify your investments across different sectors and industries. This helps reduce exposure to sector-specific risks and ensures you're not overly concentrated in any single sector.

3. Geographic Diversification: Invest in assets from different geographic regions to reduce country-specific risks and benefit from global economic growth opportunities. Geographic diversification helps spread geopolitical and currency risks.

4. Individual Asset Selection: Diversify within each asset class by selecting a mix of individual assets or securities with different risk profiles, growth prospects, and correlation to each other. Avoid overexposure to any single stock, cryptocurrency, or investment product.

5. Rebalance Regularly: Periodically review and rebalance your portfolio to maintain your desired asset allocation and risk exposure. Rebalancing involves selling assets that have appreciated in value and reinvesting the proceeds into underperforming assets to realign your portfolio with your investment objectives.

Considerations for Diversification:
1. Risk Factors: Consider the risk factors associated with each asset class, sector, or geographic region when diversifying your portfolio. Aim to achieve a balance between assets with low correlation to each other to maximize diversification benefits.

2. Investment Goals: Align your diversification strategy with your investment goals, risk tolerance, and time horizon. Your asset allocation and diversification approach may vary depending on whether you're investing for growth, income, capital preservation, or a combination of objectives.

3. Monitoring and Review: Regularly monitor and review your portfolio's performance, asset allocation, and diversification strategy. Make adjustments as needed based on changes in market conditions, economic outlook, and your personal circumstances.

Diversification is a fundamental principle of investment management that can help you manage risk, achieve more stable returns, and optimize your portfolio's risk-return profile over the long term. By diversifying wisely and staying disciplined, you can build a resilient and well-balanced investment portfolio that can weather various market conditions and uncertainties.

RISK MANAGEMENT TECHNIQUES

Effective risk management is crucial for protecting your investments and achieving long-term financial success. Here are some key risk management techniques to consider:

1. Diversification:
- **Spread Investments:** Diversify your investment portfolio across different asset classes, industries, sectors, and geographic regions to reduce the impact of individual asset or market volatility on your overall portfolio.

- **Asset Allocation:** Allocate your investment capital strategically across various asset classes, such as stocks, bonds, real estate, commodities, and cryptocurrencies, based on your risk tolerance, investment goals, and time horizon.

2. Stop-Loss Orders:
- **Define Exit Points:** Use stop-loss orders to define predetermined price levels at which you're willing to sell your investments to limit potential losses. Set stop-loss orders based on technical indicators, support levels, or percentage declines from your purchase price.

- **Discipline:** Stick to your stop-loss levels and avoid emotional decision-making. Implementing stop-loss orders helps protect your downside risk and prevents significant losses during market downturns.

3. Position Sizing:
- **Manage Exposure:** Determine the appropriate size of each investment position based on your risk tolerance and the potential impact of each position on your portfolio's overall risk and return.

- **Risk per Trade:** Limit the risk per trade to a certain percentage of your total investment capital to avoid overexposure to any single investment and maintain a diversified portfolio.

4. Risk Assessment:
- **Understand Risk Factors:** Conduct thorough risk assessments of each investment opportunity, considering factors such as market risk, credit risk, liquidity risk, geopolitical risk, and regulatory risk.

- **Risk-Reward Ratio:** Evaluate the potential risk-reward ratio of each investment to ensure that potential returns justify the associated risks. Avoid investments with unfavorable risk-reward profiles.

5. Regular Monitoring and Review:
- **Monitor Performance:** Regularly monitor the performance of your investment portfolio, individual assets, and market conditions to identify emerging risks, trends, and opportunities.

- **Review Strategy:** Periodically review your risk management strategy, investment goals, and asset allocation to ensure they remain aligned with your evolving financial situation, objectives, and risk tolerance.

6. Emergency Fund:
- **Maintain Cash Reserves:** Maintain an emergency fund or cash reserves to cover unexpected expenses, financial emergencies, or short-term liquidity needs without having to liquidate your investment portfolio at unfavorable times.

- **Financial Buffer:** Having cash reserves provides a financial buffer and peace of mind, reducing the need to take unnecessary risks or make impulsive investment decisions during turbulent market conditions.

7. Education and Research:

- Continuous Learning: Invest time in educating yourself about different investment strategies, risk management techniques, market dynamics, and economic indicators to make informed investment decisions.

- Due Diligence: Conduct thorough research and due diligence before making any investment, including analyzing financial statements, evaluating market trends, and assessing the credibility and track record of investment opportunities.

By implementing these risk management techniques and adopting a disciplined and prudent approach to investing, you can minimize downside risk, preserve capital, and increase the likelihood of achieving your long-term financial goals. Remember that risk management is an ongoing process that requires vigilance, adaptability, and a commitment to sound investment principles.

CHAPTER 5: ANALYZING ALTCOINS

FUNDAMENTAL ANALYSIS: EVALUATING PROJECTS AND TEAMS

Fundamental analysis is a method used to evaluate the intrinsic value of an asset by examining various factors that can influence its price and future prospects. When evaluating cryptocurrency projects and teams, fundamental analysis focuses on assessing the project's technology, team, community, use case, and market potential. Here's how you can conduct fundamental analysis to evaluate cryptocurrency projects and teams:

1. Project Overview:
- **Whitepaper:** Read the project's whitepaper to understand its technology, vision, goals, and underlying protocol. Pay attention to the project's mission statement, technical specifications, and roadmap for development.

- **Use Case:** Evaluate the practical application and utility of the project's technology. Assess whether the project addresses a real-world problem or offers innovative solutions to existing challenges.

2. Technology:

- Blockchain Technology: Assess the project's use of blockchain technology and its technical architecture. Evaluate factors such as scalability, security, decentralization, consensus mechanism, and interoperability with other blockchain networks.

- Codebase and Development Activity: Review the project's codebase on platforms like GitHub to assess the level of development activity, code quality, and contributions from the development team and community.

3. Team:

- Founders and Developers: Research the backgrounds, expertise, and track records of the project's founders, core developers, and key team members. Evaluate their experience in blockchain technology, relevant industries, and previous successful projects.

- Advisors and Partnerships: Consider the project's advisory board, strategic partnerships, and collaborations with reputable organizations in the blockchain and technology sectors. Assess the credibility and influence of advisors and partners.

4. Community and Governance:

- **Community Engagement:** Analyze the project's community engagement, including the size, activity level, and sentiment of its online community on platforms like Reddit, Twitter, Telegram, and Discord. Positive community sentiment and active participation can indicate strong support for the project.

- **Governance Model:** Evaluate the project's governance model and decision-making processes. Assess whether the project has transparent governance mechanisms that allow token holders to participate in protocol upgrades, voting, and decision-making.

5. Market Potential:

- **Market Demand:** Assess the market demand for the project's products or services. Evaluate factors such as target market size, competition, adoption rate, and potential for mass market appeal.

- **Token Economics:** Analyze the project's token economics, including token distribution, supply dynamics, inflation schedule, staking mechanisms, and utility within the ecosystem. Assess whether the token has intrinsic value and serves a meaningful purpose within the project's ecosystem.

6. Regulatory and Legal Considerations:

- Compliance: Evaluate the project's compliance with regulatory requirements and legal frameworks in relevant jurisdictions. Assess whether the project has taken steps to comply with Know Your Customer (KYC), Anti-Money Laundering (AML), and securities regulations.

- Legal Risks: Consider potential legal risks and regulatory uncertainties that may affect the project's operations, token issuance, and market viability. Assess whether the project has legal counsel and regulatory advisors to navigate regulatory challenges.

By conducting thorough fundamental analysis, you can gain insights into the strengths, weaknesses, opportunities, and threats of cryptocurrency projects and teams. This analysis can help you make informed investment decisions and identify promising projects with long-term growth potential in the dynamic and evolving cryptocurrency market.

TECHNICAL ANALYSIS: READING CHARTS AND INDICATORS

Technical analysis is a method used to evaluate the price movements of assets, including cryptocurrencies, by analyzing historical price data and market statistics. Reading charts and using technical indicators are key components of technical analysis. Here's how you can read charts and use indicators to analyze cryptocurrency price movements effectively:

1. Reading Charts:
- **Candlestick Charts:** Use candlestick charts to visualize price movements over time. Each candlestick represents a specific time period (e.g., one hour, one day) and displays the opening, closing, high, and low prices within that period.

- **Trend Lines:** Draw trend lines to identify the direction of the price trend. An uptrend is characterized by higher highs and higher lows, while a downtrend is characterized by lower highs and lower lows. Trend lines help identify support and resistance levels.

- **Support and Resistance Levels:** Identify key support and resistance levels where the price has historically struggled to break above (resistance) or below (support). These levels can act as barriers to price movement and provide opportunities for trading or investment decisions.

2. Using Indicators:
- **Moving Averages:** Use moving averages, such as the simple moving average (SMA) or exponential moving average (EMA), to smooth out price fluctuations and identify trends. Crossovers between different moving averages can signal changes in trend direction.

- **Relative Strength Index (RSI):** The RSI is a momentum oscillator that measures the speed and change of price movements. It ranges from 0 to 100 and indicates overbought conditions (RSI above 70) and oversold conditions (RSI below 30). Use the RSI to identify potential trend reversals or divergence between price and momentum.

- **Moving Average Convergence Divergence (MACD):** The MACD is a trend-following momentum indicator that consists of two lines: the MACD line and the signal line. Crossovers between these lines indicate changes in trend momentum. Additionally, the MACD histogram visualizes the difference between the MACD line and the signal line.

- **Bollinger Bands:** Bollinger Bands consist of a middle band (usually a moving average) and two outer bands that represent the standard deviations of price volatility. Bollinger Bands help identify overbought and oversold conditions and visualize price volatility.

3. Analyzing Chart Patterns:
- **Continuation Patterns:** Continuation patterns, such as flags, pennants, and triangles, suggest a temporary pause in the prevailing trend before resuming in the same direction. These patterns can provide opportunities for trend-following trades.

- **Reversal Patterns:** Reversal patterns, such as head and shoulders, double tops, and double bottoms, indicate a potential reversal in the prevailing trend. These patterns can signal a change in market sentiment and provide opportunities for counter-trend trades.

4. Timeframe Analysis:
- **Multiple Timeframe Analysis:** Analyze price charts across different timeframes (e.g., hourly, daily, weekly) to gain a comprehensive understanding of price trends and market dynamics. Higher time frames provide broader

trend perspectives, while lower time frames offer detailed entry and exit points.

- **Long-Term vs. Short-Term Analysis:** Consider both long-term and short-term price trends when making trading or investment decisions. Long-term analysis helps identify major trends and potential support/resistance levels, while short-term analysis helps fine-tune entry and exit points.

By combining chart reading techniques with technical indicators and pattern analysis, you can develop a comprehensive understanding of cryptocurrency price movements and make informed trading or investment decisions. Remember to practice risk management and use technical analysis as one of several tools in your trading or investment strategy.

CHAPTER 6: ADVANCED INVESTMENT METHODS

STAKING AND YIELD FARMING

Staking and yield farming are two popular methods used in the cryptocurrency ecosystem to earn passive income or rewards by participating in blockchain networks. Here's an overview of staking and yield farming, including how they work and their potential benefits:

Staking:

- **Definition:** Staking involves participating in the proof-of-stake (PoS) consensus mechanism of a blockchain network by holding and locking up a certain amount of cryptocurrency (staking tokens) to support network operations and validate transactions.

- **Validator Nodes:** Stakers, also known as validator nodes, are responsible for verifying transactions and securing the network. In return for their participation, stakers earn rewards, typically in the form of additional cryptocurrency tokens, proportional to the amount of tokens they stake.

- **Process:** To stake tokens, users typically need to hold them in a designated staking wallet or platform and participate in the network's staking mechanism according to specific rules and requirements defined by the protocol.

- **Benefits:**
  - **Passive Income:** Staking allows users to earn passive income by holding and staking their cryptocurrency tokens, similar to earning interest on traditional savings accounts.
  - **Network Participation:** Staking contributes to the security and decentralization of blockchain networks by incentivizing token holders to actively participate in network governance and consensus.

Yield Farming:
- **Definition:** Yield farming, also known as liquidity mining, involves providing liquidity to decentralized finance (DeFi) protocols or liquidity pools in exchange for rewards, such as additional cryptocurrency tokens or a share of transaction fees.

- **Liquidity Pools:** Yield farmers contribute their cryptocurrency assets to liquidity pools, which are used to facilitate trading, lending, borrowing, or other financial activities on DeFi platforms. In return, they receive rewards based on their contribution to the pool.

- **Token Pairing:** Yield farming often involves providing liquidity to specific token pairs (e.g., ETH/USDT, DAI/USDC) on decentralized exchanges (DEXs) or lending platforms, where users can earn rewards in the form of additional tokens or yields generated by the protocol.

- **Risks:**
  - **Impermanent Loss:** Yield farming carries the risk of impermanent loss, which occurs when the value of assets in a liquidity pool diverges from the value of the same assets held outside the pool due to price fluctuations.
  - **Smart Contract Risks:** Yield farming protocols are built on smart contracts, which may contain bugs or vulnerabilities that could lead to the loss of funds in extreme cases.

- **Benefits:**
  - **High Yield Potential:** Yield farming offers the potential for high yields or returns compared to traditional savings accounts or staking due to the dynamic nature of DeFi protocols and the demand for liquidity.

- **Diversification:** Yield farming allows users to diversify their cryptocurrency holdings and earn rewards by providing liquidity to various DeFi platforms and protocols.

Considerations:
- **Risk Management:** Both staking and yield farming carry inherent risks, including market volatility, smart contract vulnerabilities, and protocol risks. It's essential to assess the risks and rewards associated with each method and implement risk management strategies accordingly.

- **Research and Due Diligence:** Before participating in staking or yield farming, conduct thorough research and due diligence on the protocols, platforms, and projects involved. Consider factors such as the project's technology, team, community, security measures, and historical performance.

- **Long-Term vs. Short-Term Perspective:** Decide whether you're pursuing staking or yield farming for short-term gains or long-term investment purposes. Evaluate your investment goals, risk tolerance, and time horizon to determine the most suitable approach for your needs.

Staking and yield farming offer opportunities for cryptocurrency holders to earn passive income or rewards by actively participating in blockchain networks and DeFi ecosystems. However, it's essential to understand the associated risks and rewards and to approach these activities with caution and diligence.

LEVERAGED TRADING

Leveraged trading, also known as margin trading, allows traders to amplify their exposure to financial assets by borrowing funds from a broker or exchange. Here's an overview of leveraged trading, including how it works, its potential benefits, and associated risks:

How Leveraged Trading Works:
- **Borrowing Funds:** In leveraged trading, traders borrow funds from a broker or exchange to increase the size of their trading position beyond what they could afford with their own capital.

- **Margin Requirement:** To open a leveraged position, traders must provide collateral (margin) to cover a portion of the total value of the trade. The amount of leverage provided by the broker determines the margin requirement.

- **Leverage Ratio:** The leverage ratio represents the multiple of the trader's initial margin that they can borrow to increase their position size. Common leverage ratios include 2:1, 5:1, 10:1, or even higher, depending on the asset and the broker's policies.

- **Profit and Loss Amplification:** Leveraged trading amplifies both potential profits and losses. A small price movement in the underlying asset can result in significant gains or losses for leveraged traders, depending on the direction of the trade.

Benefits of Leveraged Trading:
- **Increased Buying Power:** Leveraged trading allows traders to control a larger position size with a smaller amount of capital. This can potentially amplify profits if the trade is successful.

- **Diversification Opportunities:** Leveraged trading provides access to a wider range of financial markets and assets, allowing traders to diversify their investment portfolio and capitalize on various market opportunities.

- **Hedging Strategies:** Traders can use leveraged trading to hedge their existing positions or portfolios by taking offsetting positions in correlated assets, thereby reducing overall risk exposure.

Risks of Leveraged Trading:
- **Increased Risk of Loss:** While leveraged trading can amplify profits, it also amplifies losses. If the market moves against the trader's position, they may incur significant losses, including the loss of their initial margin and additional funds borrowed from the broker.

- **Margin Calls and Liquidation:** If the value of the leveraged position falls below a certain threshold (maintenance margin), the broker may issue a margin call, requiring the trader to deposit additional funds to maintain the position. Failure to meet margin requirements can result in liquidation of the position, leading to further losses.

- **Volatility Risk:** Leveraged trading is particularly sensitive to market volatility. Sharp price movements in the underlying asset can trigger margin calls or liquidation events, especially in highly leveraged positions.

Risk Management Strategies:

- Position Sizing: Determine the appropriate position size based on your risk tolerance, trading strategy, and available capital. Avoid overleveraging your trades, and only use leverage that you can afford to lose.

- Stop-Loss Orders: Use stop-loss orders to limit potential losses and protect your capital. Set stop-loss levels based on your risk tolerance and the volatility of the asset being traded.

- Diversification: Spread your trading capital across multiple assets, markets, or trading strategies to mitigate concentration risk and reduce the impact of individual trade outcomes on your overall portfolio.

- Education and Research: Continuously educate yourself about leveraged trading strategies, market dynamics, and risk management techniques. Conduct thorough research and due diligence before executing leveraged trades, and stay informed about market news and developments.

Leveraged trading can be a powerful tool for experienced traders to capitalize on short-term market movements and amplify their trading returns. However, it also carries significant risks, including the potential for substantial losses. It's essential to approach leveraged trading with caution, implement robust risk management strategies, and only trade with funds that you can afford to lose.

ARBITRAGE OPPORTUNITIES

Arbitrage opportunities occur when there is a price difference for the same asset or financial instrument across different markets or exchanges, allowing traders to profit from the price discrepancy. Here's an overview of arbitrage opportunities, how they work, and the strategies involved:

How Arbitrage Opportunities Work:
- **Price Discrepancy:** Arbitrage opportunities arise when the same asset or financial instrument is priced differently across different markets, exchanges, or platforms due to factors such as market inefficiencies, geographical differences, or delays in information dissemination.

- **Buy Low, Sell High:** Arbitrageurs take advantage of the price discrepancy by buying the asset at the lower price in one market and simultaneously selling it at the higher price in another market, thereby capturing the price difference as profit.

- Market Efficiency: Arbitrage activities help drive market efficiency by aligning prices across different markets and reducing price discrepancies. As arbitrageurs exploit opportunities, they contribute to the equalization of prices and the elimination of inefficiencies.

Types of Arbitrage Opportunities:
1. Spatial Arbitrage: Spatial arbitrage exploits price differences for the same asset across different geographical regions or markets. For example, a cryptocurrency may be priced higher on one exchange than on another due to variations in supply, demand, or trading volume.

2. Temporal Arbitrage: Temporal arbitrage takes advantage of price differences for the same asset at different points in time. For example, a futures contract may be priced differently from the spot price of the underlying asset, creating arbitrage opportunities for traders who can exploit the price differential.

3. Inter-Exchange Arbitrage: Inter-exchange arbitrage exploits price differences for the same asset across different cryptocurrency exchanges. Traders buy the asset on one exchange where it is priced lower and sell it simultaneously on another exchange where it is priced higher, capturing the price discrepancy as profit.

4. Triangular Arbitrage: Triangular arbitrage involves exploiting price differences between three different currency pairs to generate profits. Traders execute a series of trades across multiple currency pairs to take advantage of inefficiencies in exchange rates.

Arbitrage Strategies:
- **Automated Trading:** High-frequency trading (HFT) algorithms and automated trading bots are commonly used to execute arbitrage strategies quickly and efficiently, leveraging technological advancements and low-latency trading infrastructure.

- **Risk Management:** Arbitrageurs must manage various risks, including execution risk, counterparty risk, and market risk. Robust risk management strategies, such as setting stop-loss orders and position limits, help mitigate potential losses.

- **Liquidity Considerations:** Arbitrage opportunities require sufficient liquidity to execute trades without significantly impacting market prices. Traders must assess liquidity conditions and trading volumes across different markets before engaging in arbitrage activities.

Considerations for Arbitrage Trading:
- **Transaction Costs:** Transaction costs, including trading fees, spreads, and slippage, can erode profits from arbitrage trades. Arbitrageurs must factor in transaction costs when evaluating the profitability of arbitrage opportunities.

- **Market Conditions:** Arbitrage opportunities may be fleeting and highly competitive, especially in efficient markets. Traders must stay vigilant and act quickly to capitalize on arbitrage opportunities before they disappear.

- **Regulatory Considerations:** Traders must comply with regulatory requirements and trading rules in different jurisdictions when engaging in arbitrage activities across multiple markets or exchanges. Failure to comply with regulations can lead to legal and regulatory issues.

Arbitrage opportunities can be lucrative for traders who can effectively identify, assess, and exploit price discrepancies across different markets or exchanges. However, arbitrage trading requires sophisticated analytical tools, advanced trading strategies, and rapid execution capabilities to capitalize on fleeting opportunities and mitigate risks effectively.

PARTICIPATING IN ICOS AND IDOS

Participating in Initial Coin Offerings (ICOs) and Initial DEX Offerings (IDOs) involves investing in newly issued cryptocurrency tokens or digital assets at their early stages of development. Here's an overview of ICOs and IDOs, including how they work, their potential benefits, and associated risks:

Initial Coin Offerings (ICOs):
- **Definition:** An ICO is a fundraising method used by blockchain projects to raise capital by issuing digital tokens or cryptocurrencies to investors in exchange for funding.

- **Token Sale:** During an ICO, investors purchase the project's tokens with established cryptocurrencies, such as Bitcoin (BTC) or Ethereum (ETH), or with fiat currencies, such as

US dollars (USD), in exchange for the newly issued tokens.

- **Use of Funds:** The funds raised through an ICO are typically used to finance the development of the project, including software development, marketing, business operations, and other expenses associated with building and launching the project.

- **Investor Participation:** Investors participate in ICOs with the expectation that the project's tokens will increase in value over time as the project progresses and achieves its milestones, potentially generating significant returns on their investment.

Initial DEX Offerings (IDOs):
- **Definition:** An IDO is a decentralized fundraising method conducted on decentralized exchanges (DEXs) or decentralized finance (DeFi) platforms, allowing projects to launch and distribute their tokens directly to investors in a decentralized manner.

- **Token Distribution:** During an IDO, tokens are typically distributed through liquidity pools or token swaps on DEXs, allowing investors to acquire the project's tokens by providing liquidity or swapping other cryptocurrencies for the newly issued tokens.

- **Decentralized Nature:** IDOs leverage the decentralized nature of blockchain technology to enable permissionless and borderless fundraising, allowing projects to reach a global audience of investors without relying on traditional intermediaries or centralized exchanges.

- **Liquidity Provision:** IDO participants may provide liquidity to liquidity pools or token pairs on DEXs in exchange for the project's tokens, thereby supporting the project's liquidity and market availability from the early stages.

Benefits of Participating in ICOs and IDOs:
- **Early Access:** Participating in ICOs and IDOs provides investors with early access to newly issued tokens at discounted prices or favorable terms, potentially allowing them to capitalize on the project's growth potential from the early stages.

- **Investment Opportunities:** ICOs and IDOs offer investment opportunities in innovative blockchain projects and decentralized applications (dApps) that aim to disrupt various industries and sectors, including finance, gaming, decentralized identity, and decentralized governance.

- Token Utility: Project tokens issued through ICOs and IDOs may have utility within the project's ecosystem, such as governance rights, access to platform services, or incentives for network participation, providing additional value to token holders.

Risks of Participating in ICOs and IDOs:
- Regulatory Risks: ICOs and IDOs may face regulatory scrutiny and legal risks due to regulatory uncertainty or non-compliance with securities laws and regulations in various jurisdictions. Investors should be aware of the regulatory landscape and potential risks associated with participating in token sales.

- Project Risks: Investing in ICOs and IDOs carries inherent risks related to the project's development, execution, and market adoption. Investors should conduct thorough due diligence on the project's team, technology, roadmap, and business model before investing.

- Market Volatility: The cryptocurrency market is highly volatile, and token prices can fluctuate significantly after the initial token sale. Investors should be prepared for price volatility and potential fluctuations in the value of their investment.

- Scam Projects: The ICO and IDO space has been associated with fraudulent or scam projects that aim to defraud investors or raise funds for non-existent or fraudulent ventures. Investors should exercise caution and skepticism and conduct thorough research to avoid falling victim to scams.

Considerations for Participating in ICOs and IDOs:

- Due Diligence: Conduct thorough research and due diligence on the project, team, technology, roadmap, community, and token economics before participating in an ICO or IDO. Evaluate the project's credibility, legitimacy, and potential for long-term success.

- Risk Management: Assess your risk tolerance and investment objectives before participating in ICOs or IDOs, and only invest funds that you can afford to lose. Diversify your investment portfolio and avoid allocating a significant portion of your capital to any single project or token sale.

- **Legal and Regulatory Compliance:** Consider the legal and regulatory implications of participating in ICOs and IDOs, including potential tax implications, securities regulations, and compliance requirements in your jurisdiction. Seek legal advice if needed to ensure compliance with applicable laws and regulations.

- **Community Engagement:** Engage with the project's community, join relevant forums, social media channels, and discussion groups, and participate in community events and initiatives to stay informed and connect with other investors and stakeholders.

Participating in ICOs and IDOs can offer investors early access to innovative blockchain projects and potential opportunities for investment growth. However, it's essential to conduct thorough research, assess the associated risks, and exercise caution when participating in token sales to make informed investment decisions.

CHAPTER 7: MANAGING AND SECURING YOUR PORTFOLIO

TRACKING INVESTMENTS AND REBALANCING

Tracking investments and rebalancing your portfolio are essential aspects of effective portfolio management, helping you monitor performance, manage risk, and maintain alignment with your investment goals and risk tolerance. Here's how you can track investments and implement rebalancing strategies:

Tracking Investments:

1. Portfolio Tracking Tools: Use portfolio tracking tools or platforms to monitor the performance of your investments in real-time, track historical returns, analyze asset allocation, and generate reports. Many brokerage firms and financial institutions offer portfolio management tools with features for tracking investments.

2. Asset Allocation: Maintain a clear understanding of your portfolio's asset allocation, including the percentage of your portfolio allocated to different asset classes, such as stocks, bonds, real estate, and cryptocurrencies. Regularly review and adjust your asset allocation based on your investment objectives and risk tolerance.

3. Performance Metrics: Evaluate the performance of individual investments and your overall portfolio using key performance metrics, such as return on investment (ROI), annualized return, volatility, Sharpe ratio, and drawdown. Compare your portfolio's performance to relevant benchmarks or indices to assess relative performance.

4. Diversification: Assess the diversification of your portfolio by analyzing the distribution of investments across different asset classes, industries, sectors, geographic regions, and investment strategies. Ensure that your portfolio is adequately diversified to mitigate concentration risk and enhance risk-adjusted returns.

5. Income and Expenses: Track the income generated by your investments, such as dividends, interest, rental income, and capital gains. Monitor investment-related expenses, including management fees, transaction costs, taxes, and other charges, to evaluate the overall cost-effectiveness of your portfolio.

Rebalancing Strategies:
1. Periodic Rebalancing: Implement a regular schedule for rebalancing your portfolio, such as quarterly, semi-annually, or annually, to realign your asset allocation with your target allocations. Rebalancing ensures that your portfolio remains aligned with your investment objectives and risk tolerance over time.

2. Threshold-Based Rebalancing: Set predefined thresholds or tolerance bands for each asset class or investment category within your portfolio. Rebalance your portfolio when the actual allocation deviates from the target allocation by a certain percentage or amount, triggering a rebalancing action.

3. Trigger Events: Use specific trigger events, such as significant market fluctuations, changes in economic conditions, or life events (e.g., retirement, college tuition), as opportunities to review and rebalance your portfolio. Adjust your asset allocation and investment strategy in response to changing market dynamics and personal circumstances.

4. Tax Considerations: Consider tax implications when rebalancing your portfolio, especially in taxable investment accounts. Minimize tax consequences by prioritizing tax-efficient strategies, such as tax-loss harvesting, asset location, and deferring capital gains realization when rebalancing.

5. Selective Rebalancing: Focus on rebalancing specific asset classes or investments that deviate significantly from their target allocations, rather than making wholesale changes to your entire portfolio. Prioritize rebalancing actions based on the magnitude of the deviation and the impact on portfolio risk and return.

Review and Adjustment:
1. Regular Review: Conduct periodic reviews of your investment portfolio to assess performance, review asset allocation, and identify rebalancing opportunities. Use these reviews as opportunities to evaluate your investment strategy, goals, and risk tolerance.

2. Adjustment: Adjust your investment strategy, asset allocation, and rebalancing approach based on changing market conditions, economic outlook, and personal circumstances. Be flexible and adaptive in response to new information, trends, and opportunities in the investment landscape.

3. Professional Advice: Consider seeking professional advice from financial advisors, portfolio managers, or investment professionals to help guide your investment decisions, develop a personalized investment strategy, and navigate complex financial markets.

Tracking investments and implementing rebalancing strategies are essential components of prudent portfolio management, helping you optimize risk-adjusted returns, maintain portfolio diversification, and achieve your long-term financial goals. By staying disciplined, proactive, and informed, you can effectively manage your investment portfolio and adapt to changing market conditions over time.

SECURING ASSETS: COLD STORAGE, TWO-FACTOR AUTHENTICATION

Securing assets is crucial in the world of cryptocurrency, where transactions are irreversible, and the risk of hacking or theft is prevalent. Cold storage and two-factor authentication (2FA) are two essential security measures for protecting your cryptocurrency assets. Here's how they work:

Cold Storage:
1. Definition: Cold storage refers to storing cryptocurrency assets offline, away from internet-connected devices, to minimize the risk of hacking or unauthorized access. Cold storage methods include hardware wallets, paper wallets, and offline storage solutions.

2. Hardware Wallets: Hardware wallets are physical devices that store cryptocurrency private keys offline. They typically come with built-in security features, such as encryption, PIN codes, and backup seeds, to protect against unauthorized access and theft. Popular hardware wallet brands include Ledger, Trezor, and KeepKey.

3. Paper Wallets: Paper wallets involve printing out the private keys and public addresses of cryptocurrency wallets on a physical piece of paper.

Paper wallets are stored in secure locations, such as safes or vaults, to prevent unauthorized access. However, paper wallets require careful handling to prevent loss or damage.

4. Offline Storage Solutions: Offline storage solutions, such as offline computers or air-gapped devices, are used to generate and store cryptocurrency private keys without internet connectivity. By keeping private keys offline, offline storage solutions mitigate the risk of online attacks and unauthorized access.

Two-Factor Authentication (2FA):

1. Definition: Two-factor authentication (2FA) adds an extra layer of security to online accounts by requiring users to provide two forms of identification to verify their identity. Common 2FA methods include SMS authentication, authenticator apps, hardware tokens, and biometric authentication.

2. SMS Authentication: SMS authentication involves receiving a one-time verification code via SMS text message to a registered mobile phone number. Users enter the verification code along with their password to authenticate their identity.

However, SMS authentication is vulnerable to SIM swapping attacks and interception.

3. Authenticator Apps: Authenticator apps, such as Google Authenticator, Microsoft Authenticator, and Authy, generate one-time verification codes that users enter along with their password to log in to their accounts. Authenticator apps are more secure than SMS authentication because they are not susceptible to SIM swapping attacks.

4. Hardware Tokens: Hardware tokens, also known as security keys or USB keys, are physical devices that generate one-time verification codes or cryptographic signatures. Users insert the hardware token into their computer or mobile device and press a button to authenticate their identity. Hardware tokens provide robust security against phishing and malware attacks.

Best Practices for Security:
1. Diversify Storage: Use a combination of cold storage and hot wallets for managing cryptocurrency assets. Keep the majority of funds in cold storage for long-term storage and only maintain a small amount of funds in hot wallets for active trading or transactions.

2. Backup and Recovery: Create secure backups of your private keys, recovery seeds, or wallet files and store them in multiple secure locations, such as safes, vaults, or safety deposit boxes. Regularly test backup and recovery procedures to ensure accessibility and integrity.

3. Regular Updates: Keep hardware wallets, software wallets, and security tools up to date with the latest firmware, software updates, and security patches to protect against known vulnerabilities and exploits.

4. Phishing Awareness: Beware of phishing attacks, fraudulent websites, and malicious emails that attempt to trick users into revealing sensitive information, such as private keys, passwords, or recovery seeds. Verify the authenticity of websites and communications before providing any personal or financial information.

By implementing cold storage solutions, such as hardware wallets and paper wallets, and enabling two-factor authentication (2FA) for online accounts, you can significantly enhance the security of your cryptocurrency assets and reduce the risk of unauthorized access, theft, or loss. Additionally, staying informed about the latest security best practices and remaining vigilant against emerging threats are essential for maintaining the integrity and safety of your cryptocurrency holdings.

CHAPTER 8: LEGAL, REGULATORY, AND TAX CONSIDERATIONS

UNDERSTANDING LEGAL FRAMEWORKS

Understanding legal frameworks is essential for navigating the regulatory landscape surrounding cryptocurrency and blockchain technology, as laws and regulations vary by jurisdiction and can impact the use, trading, and development of cryptocurrencies. Here's an overview of legal frameworks relevant to cryptocurrencies:

Regulatory Environment:
1. Securities Laws: Securities laws regulate the issuance, trading, and sale of securities, including tokens and cryptocurrencies that may be classified as securities. Compliance with securities laws typically involves registration, disclosure requirements, and investor protections to prevent fraud and ensure market integrity.

2. Anti-Money Laundering (AML) and Know Your Customer (KYC) Regulations: AML and KYC regulations require cryptocurrency businesses, including exchanges, wallets, and financial institutions, to implement customer identification and verification procedures to prevent money laundering, terrorist financing, and other illicit activities.

3. Taxation: Tax laws vary by jurisdiction and govern the taxation of cryptocurrency transactions, including buying, selling, trading, mining, and earning cryptocurrency income. Tax authorities may treat cryptocurrencies as property, assets, commodities, or currencies, subject to capital gains tax, income tax, or value-added tax (VAT).

4. Consumer Protection: Consumer protection laws aim to safeguard the rights and interests of consumers engaging in cryptocurrency transactions, including disclosures, terms of service, dispute resolution, and recourse mechanisms for addressing complaints, fraud, or misconduct.

Regulatory Bodies:
1. Financial Regulatory Authorities: Financial regulatory authorities, such as the Securities and Exchange Commission (SEC) in the United States, the Financial Conduct Authority (FCA) in the United Kingdom, and the Securities and Futures Commission (SFC) in Hong Kong, oversee the

regulation of securities, investments, and financial markets.

2. Central Banks: Central banks, including the Federal Reserve in the United States, the European Central Bank (ECB) in the Eurozone, and the Bank of Japan (BOJ), play a role in regulating monetary policy, currency issuance, and financial stability, which may indirectly affect cryptocurrencies.

3. Financial Intelligence Units (FIUs): FIUs are responsible for combating money laundering and terrorist financing by collecting, analyzing, and disseminating financial intelligence to law enforcement agencies and regulatory authorities. FIUs may require cryptocurrency businesses to comply with AML and KYC regulations.

4. Tax Authorities: Tax authorities, such as the Internal Revenue Service (IRS) in the United States, Her Majesty's Revenue and Customs (HMRC) in the United Kingdom, and the Australian Taxation Office (ATO), administer tax laws and regulations related to cryptocurrencies and enforce tax compliance.

Compliance Requirements:

1. Registration and Licensing: Cryptocurrency businesses, including exchanges, wallets, custodians, and financial services providers, may be required to register with regulatory authorities and obtain licenses or permits to operate legally within a jurisdiction.

2. Compliance Programs: Cryptocurrency businesses are often required to implement compliance programs, policies, and procedures to ensure adherence to applicable laws and regulations, including AML, KYC, and consumer protection requirements.

3. Reporting Obligations: Cryptocurrency businesses may have reporting obligations to regulatory authorities, such as submitting financial reports, transaction records, suspicious activity reports (SARs), and compliance certifications.

4. Enforcement and Penalties: Non-compliance with legal and regulatory requirements may result in enforcement actions, fines, penalties, or sanctions imposed by regulatory authorities, including civil enforcement actions, criminal prosecutions, and revocation of licenses.

International Cooperation:

1. Cross-Border Transactions: Cryptocurrencies operate across borders, requiring cooperation and coordination among international regulatory authorities to address legal and regulatory challenges, including jurisdictional issues, enforcement actions, and regulatory harmonization.

2. International Standards: International organizations, such as the Financial Action Task Force (FATF) and the International Organization of Securities Commissions (IOSCO), develop standards, guidelines, and best practices for regulating cryptocurrencies and promoting regulatory consistency and cooperation among jurisdictions.

3. Bilateral and Multilateral Agreements: Bilateral and multilateral agreements, treaties, and memoranda of understanding (MoUs) facilitate information sharing, collaboration, and mutual assistance among regulatory authorities and law enforcement agencies to combat financial crime and promote regulatory convergence.

Understanding legal frameworks and regulatory requirements is essential for cryptocurrency businesses, investors, developers, and users to ensure compliance with applicable laws, mitigate regulatory risks, and foster a supportive regulatory environment for innovation and growth in the cryptocurrency industry. Staying informed about evolving legal and regulatory developments and seeking legal advice when necessary can help navigate the complex and dynamic regulatory landscape surrounding cryptocurrencies.

TAX IMPLICATIONS OF ALTCOIN INVESTMENTS

The tax implications of altcoin investments vary depending on several factors, including your jurisdiction, the duration of your investments, and how you use your altcoins. Here's an overview of some common tax considerations for altcoin investments:

Capital Gains Tax:
1. Buying and Selling Altcoins: In many jurisdictions, including the United States, Canada, and the United Kingdom, profits from buying and selling altcoins are subject to capital gains tax. Capital gains tax is applied to the difference between the purchase price (cost basis) and the selling price of the altcoins.

2. Short-Term vs. Long-Term Capital Gains: The duration of your altcoin investment can affect the tax rate applied to your capital gains. Short-term capital gains, from investments held for one year or less, are typically taxed at higher rates than long-term capital gains, from investments held for more than one year.

3. Tax Rates: Capital gains tax rates vary by jurisdiction and can range from 0% to 40% or more, depending on your income level, filing status, and the duration of your investment. Consult with a tax professional or accountant to determine the applicable tax rates in your jurisdiction.

Trading Altcoins:
1. Frequency of Trading: If you actively trade altcoins, the profits from your trades may be treated as ordinary income rather than capital gains, depending on the frequency and volume of your trading activity. Ordinary income tax rates may apply to profits from frequent or high-volume trading.

2. Tax Reporting: Keep detailed records of your altcoin trades, including the dates of each trade, the purchase and sale prices, transaction fees, and any other relevant information. Use these records to calculate your capital gains or losses and report them accurately on your tax returns.

Mining and Staking:
1. Mining Rewards: If you mine altcoins through proof-of-work (PoW) mining, the value of the altcoins you receive as mining rewards is generally considered taxable income at the time of receipt. You may need to report mining income on your tax return and pay income tax on the value of the mined altcoins.

2. Staking Rewards: Similarly, if you earn staking rewards by staking your altcoins in a proof-of-stake (PoS) network, the value of the staking rewards is typically considered taxable income. You may need to report staking income on your tax return and pay income tax on the value of the staked altcoins.

Recordkeeping and Reporting:
1. Keep Accurate Records: Maintain detailed records of all your altcoin transactions, including purchases, sales, trades, mining rewards, staking rewards, and any other income or expenses related to your altcoin investments. Accurate record

keeping is essential for calculating your tax liability accurately.

2. Tax Reporting: Use the information from your records to report your altcoin transactions and income accurately on your tax returns. Depending on your jurisdiction, you may need to report capital gains, mining income, staking income, or other types of cryptocurrency income separately on your tax return.

Tax Deductions and Credits:
1. Transaction Fees: You may be able to deduct transaction fees, such as trading fees and mining fees, as business expenses or investment expenses on your tax return, reducing your taxable income or capital gains.

2. Tax Credits: Some jurisdictions offer tax credits or incentives for certain types of cryptocurrency activities, such as mining or staking. Check with your local tax authority to see if you qualify for any tax credits or incentives related to your altcoin investments.

Seek Professional Advice:
1. Consult with a Tax Professional: Tax laws and regulations related to cryptocurrency

investments are complex and can vary significantly by jurisdiction. Consult with a qualified tax professional or accountant who specializes in cryptocurrency taxation to ensure compliance with applicable tax laws and optimize your tax planning strategies.

2. Stay Informed: Stay informed about changes to tax laws and regulations related to cryptocurrency investments in your jurisdiction. Tax authorities are increasingly focusing on cryptocurrency taxation, and new guidance or regulations may impact your tax obligations.

Understanding the tax implications of your altcoin investments and staying compliant with applicable tax laws are essential for managing your tax liability and avoiding potential penalties or audits. By keeping accurate records, reporting your altcoin transactions accurately, and seeking professional advice when needed, you can navigate the complex tax landscape of cryptocurrency investments effectively.

NAVIGATING REGULATORY CHALLENGES

Navigating regulatory challenges in the cryptocurrency industry requires a deep understanding of the regulatory landscape, proactive compliance measures, and ongoing engagement with regulatory authorities. Here are some strategies for navigating regulatory challenges effectively:

Regulatory Landscape Analysis:

1. Jurisdictional Analysis: Understand the regulatory environment for cryptocurrencies and blockchain technology in different jurisdictions where you operate or conduct business. Regulatory requirements can vary significantly from one jurisdiction to another, impacting aspects such as licensing, compliance, and taxation.

2. Regulatory Updates: Stay informed about regulatory developments, updates, and guidance issued by regulatory authorities, government agencies, and legislative bodies. Monitor regulatory news sources, official announcements, and industry publications to track changes in regulatory requirements and compliance obligations.

3. Legal Counsel: Seek legal advice from experienced attorneys or law firms specializing in cryptocurrency law, financial regulation, and compliance. Legal counsel can provide guidance on regulatory compliance, risk mitigation strategies, and navigating complex legal frameworks.

Proactive Compliance Measures:
1. **Compliance Programs:** Develop robust compliance programs, policies, and procedures to ensure adherence to applicable laws and regulations governing cryptocurrencies, including anti-money laundering (AML), know your customer (KYC), securities laws, and tax regulations.

2. **AML/KYC Procedures:** Implement effective AML/KYC procedures to verify the identity of customers, detect and prevent money laundering, terrorist financing, and other illicit activities. Conduct due diligence on customers, monitor transactions for suspicious activity, and report any suspicious transactions to regulatory authorities as required.

3. **Licensing and Registration:** Obtain necessary licenses, permits, or registrations from regulatory authorities to operate legally within your jurisdiction and comply with licensing requirements for cryptocurrency exchanges, wallets, custodians, and other businesses.

Industry Engagement:

1. Industry Associations: Participate in industry associations, working groups, and advocacy organizations focused on promoting regulatory clarity, fostering dialogue with regulatory authorities, and advocating for favorable regulatory policies for the cryptocurrency industry.

2. Regulatory Dialogue: Engage in constructive dialogue with regulatory authorities, government officials, policymakers, and lawmakers to provide input, feedback, and expertise on regulatory issues affecting the cryptocurrency industry. Build relationships with regulators and collaborate on initiatives to address regulatory challenges.

3. Educational Outreach: Educate regulatory authorities, policymakers, and lawmakers about the benefits, opportunities, and challenges of cryptocurrencies and blockchain technology. Provide educational materials, research, and industry insights to facilitate informed decision-making and regulatory policy development.

Risk Management:

1. Risk Assessment: Conduct regular risk assessments to identify, assess, and mitigate legal, regulatory, and compliance risks associated with your cryptocurrency business operations. Evaluate potential risks related to licensing, compliance, enforcement actions, litigation, and reputational damage.

2. Compliance Monitoring: Establish procedures for ongoing compliance monitoring, internal controls, and risk management practices to monitor changes in regulatory requirements, assess compliance effectiveness, and address any compliance gaps or deficiencies promptly.

3. Contingency Planning: Develop contingency plans and response strategies to mitigate the impact of regulatory enforcement actions, investigations, or legal disputes. Prepare for various scenarios, including regulatory audits, fines, penalties, and legal challenges, and implement measures to mitigate potential adverse outcomes.

Continuous Adaptation:

1. Adaptive Compliance: Maintain agility and flexibility in your compliance approach to adapt to evolving regulatory requirements, market dynamics, and industry trends. Continuously assess and update your compliance programs, policies, and procedures to reflect changes in regulatory expectations and best practices.

2. Compliance Culture: Foster a culture of compliance within your organization by promoting awareness, accountability, and ethical behavior among employees, executives, and stakeholders. Provide training, resources, and support to empower employees to fulfill their compliance responsibilities effectively.

3. Regulatory Intelligence: Invest in regulatory intelligence tools, compliance software, and monitoring solutions to stay informed about regulatory developments, enforcement trends, and compliance risks in real-time. Leverage technology to streamline compliance processes, automate reporting, and enhance regulatory oversight.

Navigating regulatory challenges in the cryptocurrency industry requires a proactive and adaptive approach to compliance, engagement with regulatory authorities, and collaboration with industry stakeholders. By staying informed, implementing effective compliance measures, and fostering constructive dialogue with regulators, cryptocurrency businesses can navigate regulatory complexities and build trust with regulatory authorities and the broader ecosystem.

CONCLUSION

The world of cryptocurrency and blockchain technology holds immense potential to revolutionize global finance, reshape traditional business models, and empower individuals with greater financial sovereignty and inclusion. As we've explored, cryptocurrencies and blockchain-based innovations are driving fundamental changes across various sectors of the economy, from banking and finance to supply chain management and digital identity.

While the opportunities presented by cryptocurrencies are undeniable, it's essential to recognize the challenges and complexities that accompany their adoption and integration into the existing financial landscape. Regulatory uncertainty, security concerns, scalability issues, and the evolving nature of technology pose significant hurdles that must be addressed collaboratively by governments, regulatory authorities, industry stakeholders, and the broader cryptocurrency community.

Despite these challenges, the momentum behind cryptocurrency and blockchain technology continues to accelerate, fueled by growing investor interest, institutional adoption, technological advancements, and shifting paradigms in finance and economics. The emergence of decentralized finance (DeFi), non-fungible tokens (NFTs), central bank digital currencies (CBDCs), and other innovations underscores the transformative potential of this rapidly evolving ecosystem.

As we navigate the future of finance, it's imperative to foster an environment of innovation, collaboration, and responsible stewardship that balances the benefits of cryptocurrency with the need for regulatory clarity, consumer protection, and financial stability. By embracing emerging technologies, fostering inclusive growth, and navigating regulatory challenges thoughtfully, we can unlock the full potential of cryptocurrency and blockchain to create a more accessible, transparent, and resilient financial system for the benefit of all.

www.ingramcontent.com/pod-product-compliance
Lightning Source LLC
Chambersburg PA
CBHW071211240526
45470CB00018B/1711